KT-501-453

C153958509

Weapons and Armour through the Ages

Philip Parker

WAYLAND

The History Detective Investigates series:

The Celts
Anglo-Saxons
Tudor Exploration
Tudor Home
Tudor Medicine
Tudor Theatre
Tudor War
The Civil Wars
Victorian Crime
Victorian Factory
Victorian School
Victorian Transport
Local History
The Industrial Revolution
Post-War Britain
The Normans and the Battle of Hastings
Monarchs
Weapons and Armour through the Ages
Castles

First published in 2010 by Wayland

Wayland
338 Euston Road
London NW1 3BH

Wayland Australia
Level 17/207 Kent Street
Sydney, NSW 2000

Editor: David John
Designer: Darren Jordan
Consultant: Andy Robertshaw

British Library Cataloguing in Publication Data:
Parker, Philip.
Weapons and armour through the ages. -- (The history detective investigates)
1. Armor--History--Juvenile literature. 2. Weapons--History--Juvenile literature.
I. Title II. Series
355.8'09-dc22

ISBN: 978-0-7502-6229-3

Printed in China

Wayland is a division of Hachette Children's Books, an Hachette UK company

Picture Acknowledgments: Front cover left Denisenko/Dreamstime.com; front cover right standby/iStockphoto.com; 1 Dzain/Dreamstime.com; 2 Razvanjp/Dreamstime.com; 4 Travel Ink/Getty Images; 5t Biserko/Dreamstime.com; 5b Johnny Shumate/Public Domain; 6 jgroup/iStockphoto.com; 7t bbstanicic/iStockphoto.com; 7b cbsva/iStockphoto.com; 8 Keeshu/GNU ShareAlike; 9t Gary Ombler/Getty Images; 9b Argestes/Dreamstime.com; 10 Geoff Dann/Getty Images; 11t Public Domain; 11b Nantela/Dreamstime.com; 12 and 13t Bruno Morandi/Getty Images; 13b Public Domain; 14 MLenny/iStockphoto.com; 15l dbtale/Dreamstime.com; 15r Ruprecht Heller/Getty Images; 16 Public Domain; 17t Razvanjp/Dreamstime.com; 17b Echoart/Dreamstime.com; 18 Ernest Crofts/Getty Images; 19t Creative Commons Attribution ShareAlike; 19c and 19b Mccool/Dreamstime.com; 20 Warner Bros./Getty Images; 21t Joeygil/Dreamstime.com; 21b Public Domain; 22l Mccool/Dreamstime.com; 22r GNU ShareAlike; 23t Gatordawg/Dreamstime.com; 23b Public Domain; 24 Public Domain; 25t Jeff Kubina/Creative Commons Attribution ShareAlike; 25b Mccool/Dreamstime.com; 26 Shane T McCoy/Public Domain; 27t and 27b Public Domain; 28 igs942/iStockphoto.com; 29t Pradi/Dreamstime.com; 29b Dzain/Dreamstime.com.

Above: A Japanese samurai warrior wore a mask to strike fear into his enemies.
Previous page: In the ancient Roman military formation known as the *testudo*, or tortoise, foot soldiers used their shields to create a defensive wall.

Contents

Words in **bold** can be found in the glossary on page 30.

The history detective Sherlock Bones will help you to find clues and collect evidence about weapons and armour. Wherever you see one of Sherlock's paw-prints, you will find a mystery to solve. The answers can be found on page 31.

What weapons did ancient peoples fight with?

Weapons are the deadly tools people have used through the ages to attack their neighbours and rivals. Armour is what they have used to protect themselves against attack. The very first weapons were the bow, spear and club, which were originally invented for hunting.

At first, weapons were made of wood, stone or bone, but slowly the metal bronze came into use. About 5,000 years ago people were starting to build large cities to live in. It was then that they also started to create armies to defend their cities. By 3,000 years ago, iron had replaced bronze. Iron is harder than bronze and allowed the production of the first really effective swords.

A carving at the Great Temple of Abu Simbel, Egypt, shows Pharaoh Ramesses II fighting in a chariot during the Battle of Kadesh in 1274 BCE.

From the seventh century BCE, the people of ancient Greece developed a new system of states based around single cities. They also had a new sort of heavily armed warrior – the hoplite. A hoplite wore thick bronze armour. The cuirass covered their body, while their legs were protected by pieces of armour called greaves. They wore many different kinds of helmet. One kind, called a Corinthian, was made from a single sheet of bronze that protected their whole head, with a long projection to cover their neck and large eye slits. The hoplites carried a long, round shield (called a *hoplon*), a long spear and a short sword called a *xiphos*. They fought in a formation, normally eight rows of men deep, called a **phalanx**. This created a wall of shields that was very hard for enemies to penetrate.

A bronze Corinthian helmet (above) offered great protection but restricted the wearer's hearing and vision.

In the fourth century BCE, under Alexander the Great, the Macedonian Greeks started to use a longer spear, called a *sarissa*, which was up to 7 m (23 ft) long. The sarissa was very hard to hold, but made sure that enemies on foot could get nowhere near the Macedonian phalanx.

This illustration of a fourth-century BCE hoplite (left) shows him wielding a *sarissa*.

Detective work

The Greek hoplites defeated a huge invading Persian army in 490 BCE. Which long-distance running race is named after the battle, and why?

What weapons were used by ancient Egyptian charioteers?

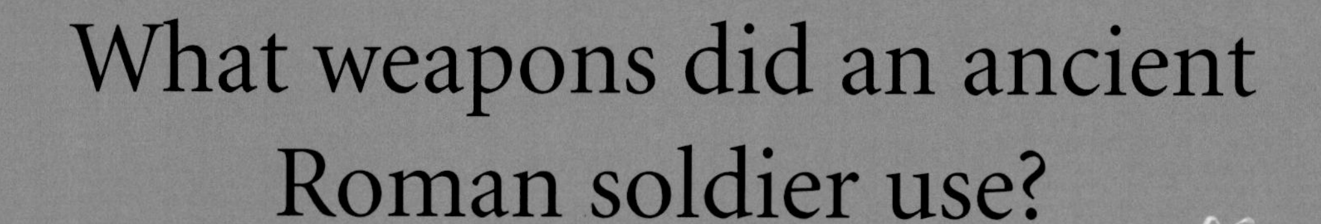

What weapons did an ancient Roman soldier use?

The Roman empire was the most powerful and farthest reaching that the world had ever seen. To conquer and then to defend such an empire needed an equally huge army. At its peak, the Roman army numbered nearly 400,000 men. This army was made up of professional soldiers whose training and equipment made them feared by their enemies.

The Romans originally fought in phalanxes, like the Greeks (see page 5), but by the second century BCE their fighting unit was called the legion. Each legion was made up of about 5,000 soldiers, who fought on foot. Each soldier, or legionary, served in the army for 25 years. There were also specialist groups in the Roman army made up of archers, **slingsmen** (who fired stones from small slings) or **artillery** units, which used large **catapults** to hurl stones and bolts at the enemy.

One of the main weapons of the Roman legionary was the *pilum*, a thin-shafted javelin whose sharp point could pierce armour. Its iron shank – the part between the point and the **shaft** – was designed to bend on impact with the shield of an enemy, making it impossible for the enemy to hurl it back. Most legionaries would carry two javelins, but for close-up, hand-to-hand fighting they needed other weapons. Most had a short sword (*gladius*) and a dagger (*pugio*). The legionary's shield (*scutum*) was a curved wooden rectangle with an iron boss (or knob) in the middle which itself could be used as a weapon to strike at enemies.

A Roman *optio* was second-in-command of the century, or group of 100 legionaries, in which he served.

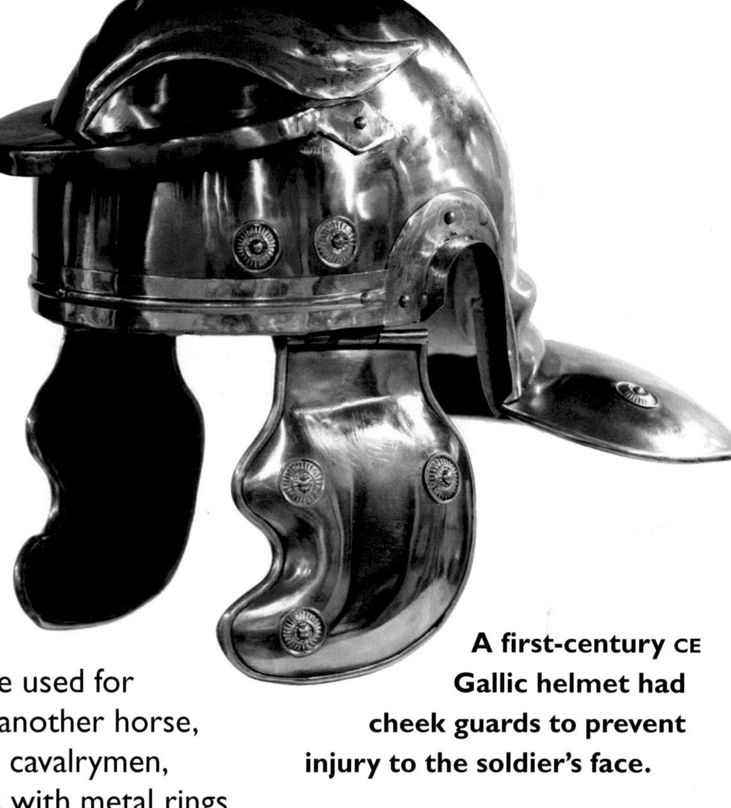

Roman legionaries wore many different kinds of armour, but the most well known was called *lorica segmentata*, made of sheets of overlapping iron plates that covered the soldier's body and part of his arms. Although strong, the plates were flexible enough to allow good freedom of movement. Helmets came in a variety of shapes, but one of the most common styles was the Gallic, an iron helmet with a large plate to protect the neck and long cheek guards.

From the third century CE, the **cavalry**, or horseback soldiers, became more important to the Roman army. Many soldiers now carried a longer sword (*spatha*), which could be used for reaching enemies on the ground or seated on another horse, and shields became smaller and rounder. Some cavalrymen, called *cataphracts*, wore long **chain mail** coats with metal rings sewn into them. Their helmets looked like a round bowl with cheek pieces and a metal ridge on top.

A first-century CE Gallic helmet had cheek guards to prevent injury to the soldier's face.

This recreation shows various Roman weapons, from a shield to a bow and arrows.

DETECTIVE WORK

The Roman short sword (*gladius*) came from the region the Romans called Hispania (modern-day Spain and Portugal). To find out how other Roman weapons developed, try www.roman-colosseum.info/roman-weapons/index.htm

How might a legionary spot his officers in the thick of battle?

Why were people so afraid of the Vikings?

Early in the ninth century CE, raiders from Scandinavia (modern-day Denmark, Sweden and Norway) started to attack towns along the coasts of northern and western Europe. These raiders are known as Vikings, and for just over 200 years they spread fear wherever they went. Viking warriors were experienced and terrifyingly effective fighters. A major Viking raid might have 100 ships, each containing around 50 warriors.

'Never before has such terror arisen … nor was it before considered that such an inroad could be made from the sea.'

Alcuin of York, on the Viking attack on the monastery of Lindisfarne (in modern-day north-east England) in CE 793.

The Vikings' most effective weapons were their speedy **longships**. These ships were specially designed with shallow hulls, or bodies, so that they could sail close to the coast and even up rivers. This meant the Vikings did not need ports and they could attack a much wider area. The Vikings were also skilled metal-workers. They carried a variety of slashing swords, spears and, above all, long axes that had to be wielded with two hands.

Why did poorer Viking warriors use an axe rather than a sword?

Viking armour depended on the warrior. The richest Vikings carried round wooden shields and wore chain mail coats and metal helmets, which were often bowl-shaped. The poorer Vikings might have only padded leather jackets, spears and long knives (*saxes*). One group of Viking warriors, called 'berserkers', fought with no armour other than animal skins. Berserkers made up for their lack of protection with an aggression that terrified their enemies.

This Viking sword pommel, which forms part of the handle, is made of metal and decorated with twisting chains.

These replicas show the range of Viking axes. On the left is a medium-weight axe. The axe on the right is for throwing.

DETECTIVE WORK

Traditional pictures of the Vikings show them with horned helmets. Look at examples of Viking armour that have been found. Did they really have helmets with horns?

In battle, the Vikings often formed up behind a wall of shields, from where they could hurl spears, shoot arrows or cast **slingshots** against their enemies before charging. The warriors were very mobile, able to retreat to their ships and sail away if a battle was not going well.

From the late ninth century CE, Vikings set sail in greater numbers and settled down in northern France, Ireland, England and Scotland, establishing kingdoms there. They also made settlements in Iceland and Greenland, and sent expeditions to North America around CE 1000, making them the first Europeans known to have reached that continent.

The Viking warriors continued to be feared for their strength in battle, but once they had formed their new settlements, they were forced to defend their fields and towns, just as the Vikings' victims had had to do. By the late eleventh century, the longships stopped sailing from Scandinavia, and the fierce Viking warrior became a figure known only in traditional Viking tales, called sagas.

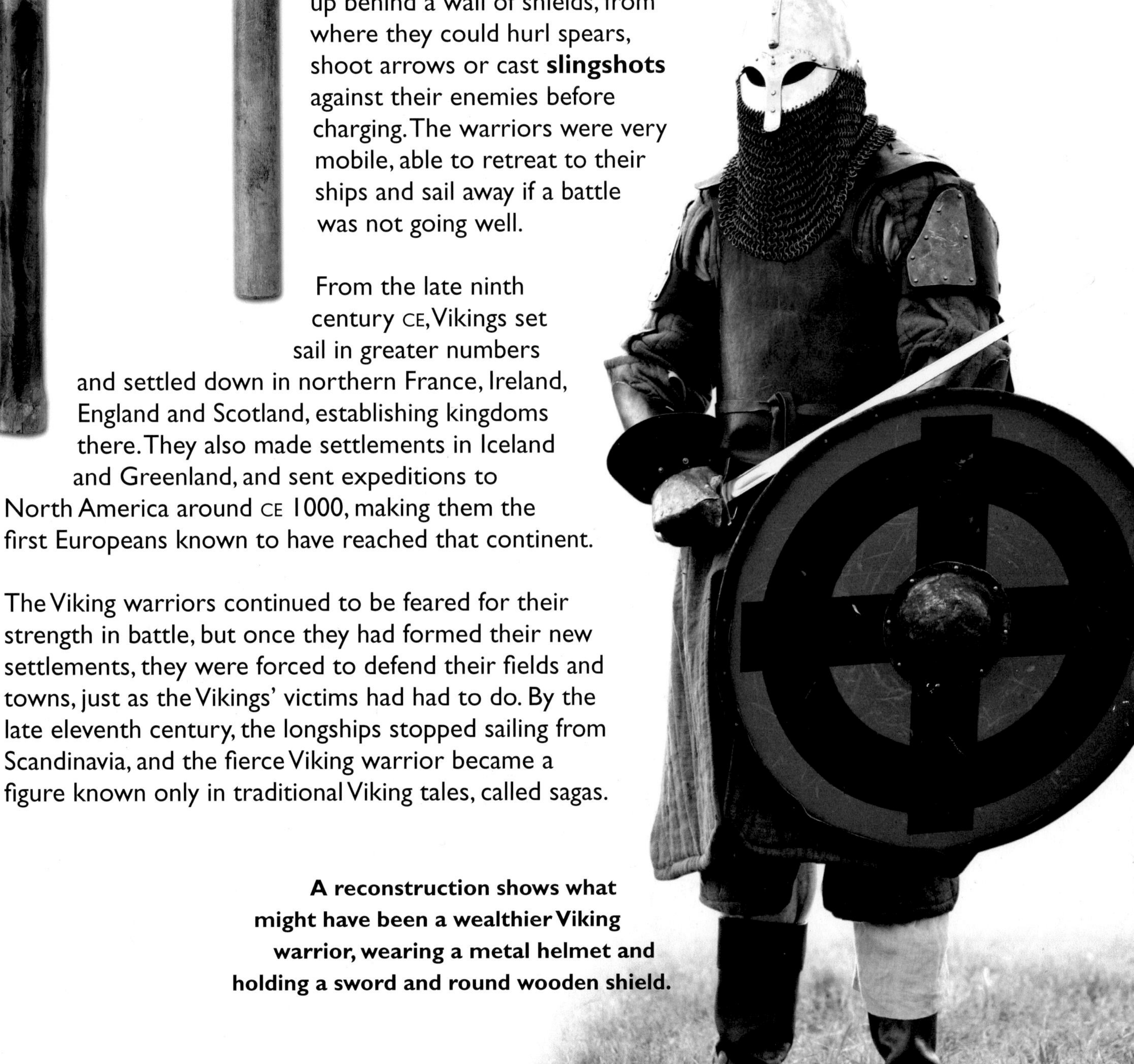

A reconstruction shows what might have been a wealthier Viking warrior, wearing a metal helmet and holding a sword and round wooden shield.

Why did medieval knights wear such heavy armour?

By the Middle Ages, weapons had become so effective that knights had to protect themselves from head to foot inside a suit of armour. From the ninth and tenth centuries, the most respected type of warrior in Europe was the knight, or a fighter mounted on horseback.

Knights were not normal soldiers. Ordinary people were not allowed to become knights. In any case, only the rich could afford to keep the horses a knight needed, or to buy the weapons and armour. Knights started training as young boys, when they were called pages, and served for a time as the assistant (or squire) to a knight, before becoming knights themselves.

Under the system known as **feudalism**, which was common in western Europe in the Middle Ages, knights were given land by a lord. In return, they served in the lord's army for a number of days each year. The great lords held their land from the king and had to provide a certain number of knights for his army. These armies were made up of a large number of knights and their retainers (followers) and a less well-trained group of foot soldiers.

The knights' main weapon was the sword, which was light enough to be used on horseback. In the thirteenth century, larger swords appeared, often called 'great swords', with blades over 1 m (3 ft) long. Although more comfortable to hold in two hands, they could still be used in one. Knights also used a variety of other weapons, such as **maces** and war-hammers (which had a hammer-shaped piece to stun enemies, as well as a sharp, pick-shaped blade to inflict cuts).

DETECTIVE WORK

In the Battle of Hastings in 1066, Bishop Odo of Bayeux used a mace as his weapon. Find out why at www.bayeuxtapestry.org.uk/BayeuxPeople.htm

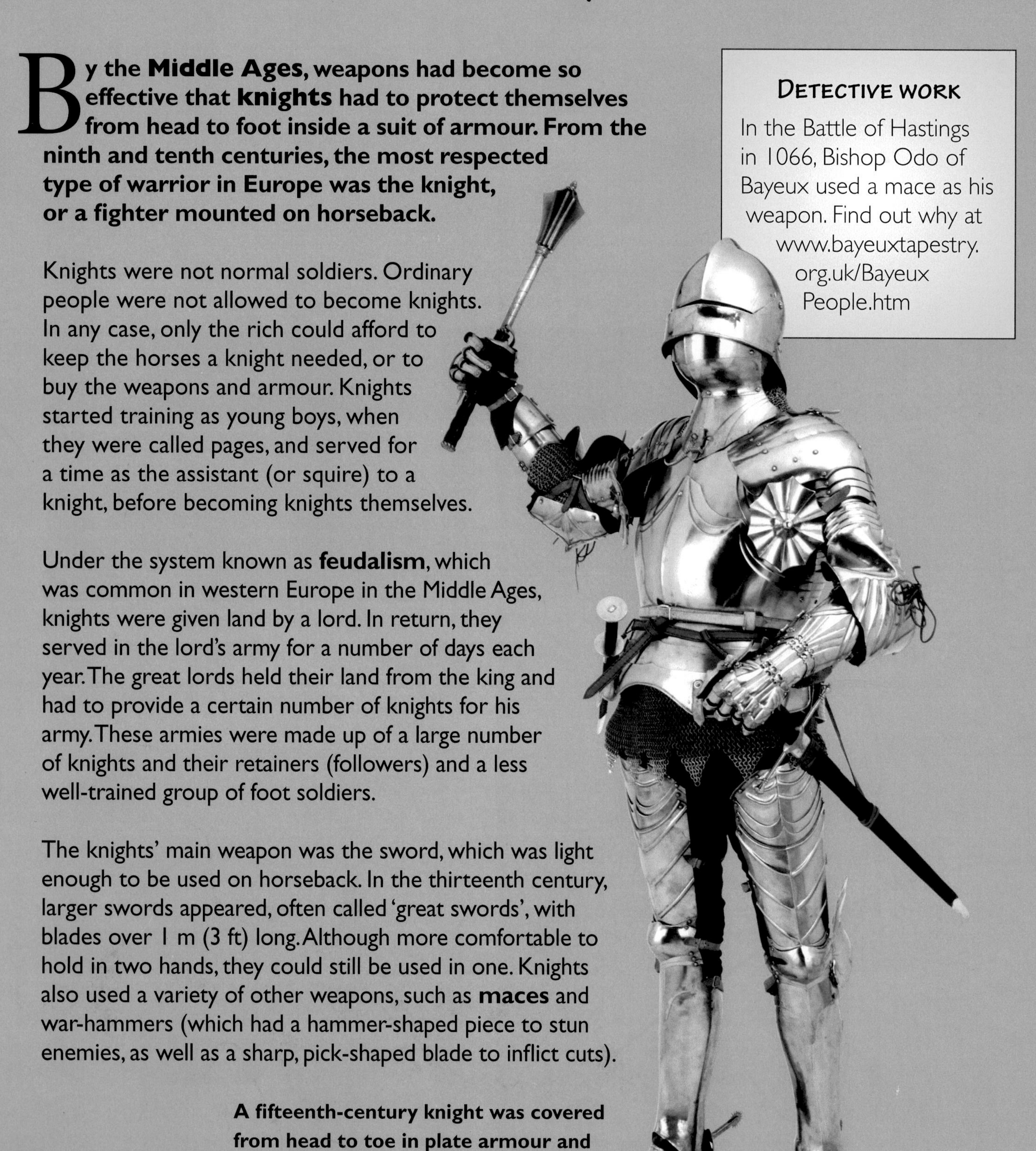

A fifteenth-century knight was covered from head to toe in plate armour and might wield a mace as well as a sword.

At first, the knight's armour was similar to chain mail, but over time it became heavier. Solid metal plates (sections made from one piece of metal) were added to cover parts of the body such as the chest, groin or legs. Finally, in the fifteenth century, full plate armour was introduced, which covered almost the whole of the knight's body. Helmets also became more complicated. They started with a simple metal head-covering and cheek guard and ended with a case that completely covered the head, with only a narrow visor so that the knight could see out. Arrows and swords would rarely hurt a knight wearing such full armour and a helmet.

A fifteenth-century illustration shows a knight striking with his great sword. It is so heavy that he is using both hands to wield it.

To attack a knight, foot soldiers would try to pull him off his horse and kill him on the ground. Foot soldiers of the Middle Ages were armed with clubs, spears, some swords and even tools taken from farms. Armies also had archers known as longbowmen, who shot arrows from a **longbow**. The English longbowmen were especially skilled. They could shoot arrows at ranges of up to 200 m (650 ft). Medieval armies also had large numbers of crossbowmen, using a weapon similar to a bow but shooting a bolt which was released after a winding **mechanism** had been cranked. The bolts from crossbows were one of the few things that could penetrate plate armour and kill a knight from a distance.

Why did knights need to have a squire to help them?

In the later Middle Ages, knights and foot soldiers might have used a spiked flail to strike their enemies.

Why were Mongol bows and arrows so deadly?

In the thirteenth century, a group of peoples from Central Asia called the Mongols united under a single ruler named Genghis Khan. The Mongols were nomads, who travelled great distances on horseback, bringing their families and herds of animals with them. They were also skilled warriors, using special bows that could shoot longer distances than those of their enemies.

> *'Heaven has promised me victory.'*
>
> Mongol ruler Genghis Khan.

Under Genghis Khan, the Mongols conquered Central Asia, northern China and most of Russia by 1240. They then moved farther west, devastating large parts of Poland and Hungary. At their most powerful, the Mongols ruled all the lands from modern-day China, through Russia to eastern Europe.

The Mongols were expert cavalrymen who could shoot off arrows while riding at full speed on their horses. They would carry several bows in case the string of one of them broke.

Why could Mongol horsemen travel faster than European knights?

This re-enactment (below) shows Mongol warriors wearing metal helmets and tough leather armour.

A modern-day Mongol archer uses a traditional bow similar to that wielded by his ancestors.

Their main weapon was known as the composite bow. The bow had a wooden frame covered in layers of bone and horn, which gave it greater strength and pulling power than a simple wooden bow. The composite bow had a range of up to 300 m (980 ft), compared to the 200-m (650-ft) range of their enemies' finest bows. This meant that the Mongols could hit their opponents before the enemy had any chance to reach them with an arrow. The Mongols would then pull back as the enemy tried to make an attack, shooting off more arrows. Only when their enemy was weakened would the Mongols **charge**, using weapons such as swords and maces to finish them off.

Mongol armour was made of hardened plates of leather sewn together, which allowed their warriors freedom of movement. As time passed, the Mongols also started to use some of the weapons of the peoples they had conquered, particularly the Chinese. These included catapults that threw bolts and stones.

Detective work

What unusual drink did the Mongols use to keep them going on long rides? Find out at http://www.coldsiberia.org/monmight.htm

In 1299, the Mongols, armed with bows (the group on the left in this picture), defeated the Mamluks (right) near Homs in modern-day Syria.

How did weapons change after the invention of gunpowder?

By the early 1500s, the heavy plate armour of the knights was becoming less effective on Europe's battlefields. This was because gunpowder had arrived. Gunpowder had been invented in China in the ninth century CE. It was an explosive mixture of charcoal, potassium nitrate and sulphur.

The Chinese were the first to use gunpowder as a weapon, placing it in bamboo tubes and setting light to it to make flames or stone balls fly out of the tube. By the early fourteenth century, European armies were using gunpowder in cannons, metal tubes that shot out stone or metal balls. In the earliest cannons, a stone or metal ball was simply pushed into the **barrel** with a small amount of gunpowder, which was then lit through a hole in the top of the barrel. The gunpowder exploded, hurling the ball out. Sometimes the cannon exploded, too.

By the seventeenth century, the musket had become the standard weapon of European foot soldiers.

Early guns were very heavy and could not be moved about easily. The first guns that could be carried around by soldiers appeared in the 1420s and were like small cannons on the end of long **pikes** stuck in the ground. By the 1470s, these had developed into the first practical hand gun, known as the arquebus. It had a metal barrel attached to a wooden stock (or handle), which could be propped against the soldier's shoulder when firing.

Detective work

After the invention of gunpowder, soldiers stopped wearing heavy armour, but over time they stopped using another weapon, too. Can you work out which weapon it was and why?

At first, guns played only a small part in battles. In most armies, cavalrymen still wore heavy armour and carried swords or **lances**. Foot soldiers had a variety of hand-held weapons. But things began to change in the 1400s. **Infantry** from Switzerland started carrying very long pikes – up to 6 m (20 ft) long – which the enemy's cavalry could not charge. The Swiss mixed soldiers carrying arquebuses in with these pikemen. The guns were very slow to reload, but protected behind the line of pikes, this could be done in safety.

Where did musketeers keep the ammunition for their muskets?

At the Battle of Pavia in Italy, in 1525, guns won a battle for the first time, as arquebusiers (soldiers armed with arquebuses) fired at Francis I of France's army and caused it to run away. Smaller weapons that could be used by cavalry, such as **pistols**, appeared from the 1540s. By the early 1600s, lighter versions of the arquebus, called **muskets**, had become the standard weapon of foot soldiers. As guns were now more powerful, the bullets they shot out could penetrate even the best armour, so most soldiers stopped wearing it.

The pike is a very long spear, held as a defence against charges by foot soldiers and cavalry.

Weapons such as cannons and pikes were used beside arquebuses at Pavia in 1525.

Why was the Japanese samurai sword so special?

The traditional Japanese sword, the *katana*, is one of the finest weapons ever designed. It was wielded by a special type of Japanese warrior known as a samurai. The samurai lived by a strict code of behaviour, called *bushido*. This set down not just how they should fight but how they should always behave with loyalty and honour. If a samurai did something that broke this code, he might choose to kill himself rather than face dishonour.

'It is not the way of the warrior to be shamed and avoid death even under circumstances that are not particularly important. It goes without saying that to sacrifice one's life for the sake of his master is an unchanging principle.'

Torii Mototada, samurai general, before his death at the Siege of Fushima, 1600.

From the twelfth century, the emperors of Japan lost power to new military rulers, called shoguns. In the period of warring that followed, the samurai started to emerge. These mounted fighters played a similar role in Japanese society to that of the knights in western Europe, with great lords having a band of samurai sworn to their service.

What were the main weapons used at the Battle of Shiroyama?

In 1877, a group of samurai fought the government at the Battle of Shiroyama.

The masks worn by samurai warriors were often painted bright colours to scare the enemy.

The *katana*, made of layers of steel which gave it great strength, flexibility and sharpness, could only be carried by samurai. Non-samurai soldiers could carry a shorter sword, the *wakizashi*, but this was much less effective than the *katana*. Samurai also carried short daggers (*tanto*), used for close combat. Their *yari* was a spear with a straight blade which could be up to 6 m (20 ft) long.

Samurai armour could be highly decorated. It was made up of plates of metal or leather, held together by leather lacing. It was light and allowed easy movement when sword-fighting. The helmet often had imitation buffalo horns on top, and the samurai also wore a mask to make them even more frightening.

In the sixteenth century, leading Japanese lords fought each other in a series of wars which led to the unification of Japan. For the first time, large numbers of samurai carried guns. After Japan became a unified country, there was no longer any reason to have large armies. The samurai no longer needed to fight, although they remained very important in Japanese society. As they became more government officials than warriors, their armour became even more splendid, but they rarely had reason to use their *katana*.

Detective work

The samurai warrior kept his gold in a safe place. Can you work out where this was? (Clue: look at the handles of the swords.) The samurai age came to an end in 1868. Can you find out why? Try using books from your school or local library or looking on the Internet.

The samurai's *katana* was so precious to him that it was considered to be a living thing and often given a name.

What were the winning weapons in the Battle of Waterloo?

From 1805 to 1815, the French emperor Napoleon Bonaparte fought a series of wars with his European neighbours. Huge armies, sometimes numbering over 100,000 men, criss-crossed Europe in what came to be known as the Napoleonic Wars. Finally, in 1815, the armies of Britain, Prussia (now in Germany) and their allies defeated Napoleon at the Battle of Waterloo.

Cavalry soldiers at Waterloo were equipped with **carbine** guns, which had been developed in the eighteenth century. The carbine was shorter than the old musket, which made it easier to handle. It was also much quicker to reload. The use of the rifle by specialist, sharp-shooting troops also became more widespread. Curved grooves on the inside of the barrel, known as 'rifling', made the bullet more stable as it was shot out. This made rifles more accurate than muskets over longer distances.

Most foot soldiers at Waterloo still carried **smooth-bored** (non-rifled) muskets. The most common weapon on the British side was a type of musket known as the 'Brown Bess'. Soldiers fired in **volleys** (when many soldiers fired at once). This was designed to cause maximum enemy injuries, but only half the shots fired at 125 m (400 ft) would hit a target.

Detective work

The bayonet became a very important weapon for infantry fighting at close range in this period. Can you find out exactly how it was used? Try http://thearmouryonline.co.uk/BayonetHistory.htm

In an 1879 painting, a defeated Napoleon (grey coat, centre) is seen exiting his carriage among his confused troops.

Each side at the Battle of Waterloo used a lot of artillery – large cannons that were pulled by horses. These caused many deaths and injuries. When the fighting started, the infantry formed up in lines, mostly two deep, with one line firing their muskets while the other reloaded. If charged by enemy cavalry, the infantry formed up into a square which the horses found difficult to break into. The infantry were also armed with **bayonets**, long daggers which slotted into a socket on the end of a gun. They would use the bayonet to stab at enemy soldiers.

Unlike soldiers of earlier times, the infantry at Waterloo wore little armour, which would have been no use against musket or rifle shots. Soldiers now wore uniforms to tell their own side from the enemy. National uniform colours, such as French Blue and British Red, were used to differentiate the armies.

The cavalry played a large role in the Napoleonic Wars. They could move quickly across the battlefield and pursue fleeing enemy soldiers. They often carried a **sabre**, a light, curved sword used for slashing or thrusting. The role of the heavy cavalry, or cuirassiers, was to fight hand-to-hand with the enemy. They wore a metal breastplate (or cuirass) and carried a heavy, long sword and pistol (a small hand-held gun). The light cavalry was used for communications and sudden raids. They did not wear heavy armour and usually carried a carbine or musket. Another type of cavalry was the lancers. Like medieval knights, they carried long lances to charge the enemy. The lancers were the only form of cavalry that could easily break through enemy infantry squares.

A cuirassier's helmet had a horse-hair plume.

The Brown Bess musket (above) was used by the British infantry at Waterloo.

A French cuirassier's steel breastplate (above) offered protection against sword cuts.

How were cannon usually transported on nineteenth-century battlefields?

Why were rifles so important in the US Civil War?

In 1861, fighting broke out between the Northern and the Southern states of America. The war was fought mainly over slavery, which Southerners wanted to keep but Northern politicians were trying to ban, or abolish. Northerners were known as Unionists, while Southerners were known as Confederates. The large armies on both sides needed mass-produced firearms in numbers never seen before.

Firearms were now much more accurate – and effective at greater distances – than those used in the Napoleonic Wars. Foot soldiers could be shot down long before they had a chance to reach the enemy. The best rifles could hit their target at about 600 m (2,000 ft). A new percussion cap system for firing was now used in most guns. A hammer struck the explosive charge, sending a spurt of flame into the barrel and pushing out the bullet. This was safer and more reliable than the old system in which a flint (or stone) set light to the gunpowder.

DETECTIVE WORK

The Northern states wanted to ban slavery in America, and many African-Americans fought on that side in the Civil War. Around 198,000 served in the army and navy. Even on the Union side, however, black soldiers faced discrimination. To find out more, try http://history-world.org/black_regiments.htm

In this re-enactment, Confederate soldiers take over a Union camp.

Historical re-enactors (right), dressed as Union soldiers, fire carbines.

Famous American gunmakers such as Samuel Colt had been busy developing better hand guns before the Civil War. Colt's revolver hand gun had a cylinder with several holes in which the bullets were placed. When a bullet was fired, the cylinder would revolve, or turn, to make the next bullet ready without reloading. New breech-loading rifles were also introduced, in which the bullet was placed at the back of the barrel rather than pushed down the **muzzle**.

Cartridges, which had the explosive charge packed in with the bullet, made reloading and firing such weapons much easier. The breech-loading Spencer rifle was so effective that, by the end of the war, the Union side had ordered more than 100,000 of them. More old-fashioned muskets, such as the Springfield, were still used by the Confederates. Both armies used a variety of pistols and revolvers, many of them Colt-designed models.

Soldiers on both sides used bayonets for close fighting, and the cavalry were equipped with sabres. But these weapons caused very few casualties compared to the huge numbers of deaths inflicted by firearms. In 1863, the Battle of Gettysburg was a victory for the North and started their slow defeat of the South. During the battle, 5,000 Southerners died in one charge alone. They were cut down by rifle fire.

In battle Confederate troops sometimes used their own personal hunting rifles, such as the Hawken (below).

What did the stars on the Confederate flag represent?

Which invention killed millions of soldiers in the First World War?

The First World War (1914–18) was deadlier than any previous conflict, killing 15 million people. It began in Serbia, in south-eastern Europe, but it spread rapidly. In western Europe, Germany and its allies faced Britain, France and their allies. The war soon settled into a bloody stalemate, in which neither side could gain ground. Both sides dug systems of trenches, or ditches, which it was very difficult for the other side to storm. Only in 1918 were the Germans pushed back and forced to sign an armistice, or ceasefire.

It was the invention of the machine gun that had a terrifying effect on the fighting in the First World War. The earliest form of the machine gun, the Gatling gun, was designed in 1862. Its First World War successors automatically shot out bullets from swiftly turning barrels that could fire up to 600 rounds a minute. As troops tried to cross the ground between the two sides' trenches (known as no-man's-land), they were slaughtered in great numbers by enemy machine-gunners.

Invented in 1884, the Maxim gun (below) could fire up to 600 rounds of bullets a minute.

DETECTIVE WORK

One German variety of a common First World War weapon was nicknamed 'the potato masher' by the British. What was it? Try www.inert-ord.net/ger03a/gerhgr/stck

German machine-gunners and sentries sometimes wore heavy metal body armour.

The Mills bomb (above) was adopted as the British army's standard hand grenade in 1915.

On the first day of the Battle of the Somme in northern France, 1 July 1916, nearly 20,000 British soldiers were killed by German machine guns. By the end of the war, millions of men on both sides of the conflict had been killed by machine guns.

Ordinary First World War soldiers still carried traditional firearms. At the start of the war, most foot soldiers were armed with bolt-action rifles. In these, the soldier pulled a lever which operated a bolt. The bolt opened the back of the gun's barrel, ejecting the old shell or cartridge case of the bullet that had just been fired, so making reloading easier. Bolt-action rifles had first been made in the 1820s, but First World War models such as the Lee-Enfield (British) and Mauser (German) could fire accurately at much longer distances. A few self-loading rifles were developed during the war. In these, a magazine (which stored and fed bullets) attached to the gun delivered the next cartridge without the soldier needing to reload. Most rifles were fitted with bayonets.

Other weapons included the first **hand grenades**. From 1915, the British used the pineapple-shaped Mills bomb. But in this war, artillery was even more important than before, with heavy artillery fire being used before most attacks by foot soldiers. Other mechanised weapons came into use, such as the tank, which was first used in 1916 during the Battle of the Somme, and aircraft, which were used both for bombing and attacking enemy planes.

'It was a magnificent display of trained and disciplined valour, and its assault only failed of success because dead men can advance no further.'

General Beauvoir de Lyle on the Canadian Newfoundland Regiment at the Battle of the Somme, 1916.

What did troops wear over their faces for protection from another type of terrifying weaponry?

The Vickers machine gun needed a team of up to eight men to operate it. One man fired, one loaded ammunition and the rest carried the gun.

What kinds of weapons were used on D-Day?

On 6 June 1944, Allied armies landed in northern France – on the day they were calling D-Day. They were launching a massive attack aimed at freeing Europe from German occupation. The Allies involved in D-Day were British, American, Canadian, French, Polish and Norwegian. Germany had started the Second World War in 1939, when they had invaded Poland, but the fighting drew in countries from every continent. Following the D-Day landings, Allied troops pushed on into Germany, while Soviet forces advanced on the Germans from the east. Germany was forced to surrender in 1945.

At the beginning of the war, the opposing armies had been armed with rifles similar to those used in the First World War. The standard British weapon was the Rifle No. 4, while the Germans mostly carried a Mauser, the Karabiner 98K. When the Americans joined the war in 1941, their main infantry weapon was the M1 Garand semi-automatic rifle, which had a range of about 400 m (1,300 ft). More than 4 million Garand rifles had been produced by the end of the war. More effective still was the M1 carbine.

DETECTIVE WORK

The most effective German machine gun on D-Day was the MG34, which could fire around 800 rounds a minute. It was nicknamed the 'Spandau' by the British. Why was this? Try searching for the MG34 at ww2db.com

On D-Day, German forces used weapons ranging from stick hand grenades (shown below) to rifles, pistols, submachine guns, flame throwers and anti-tank rockets.

What animal was used as the symbol, or insignia, of Nazi Germany?

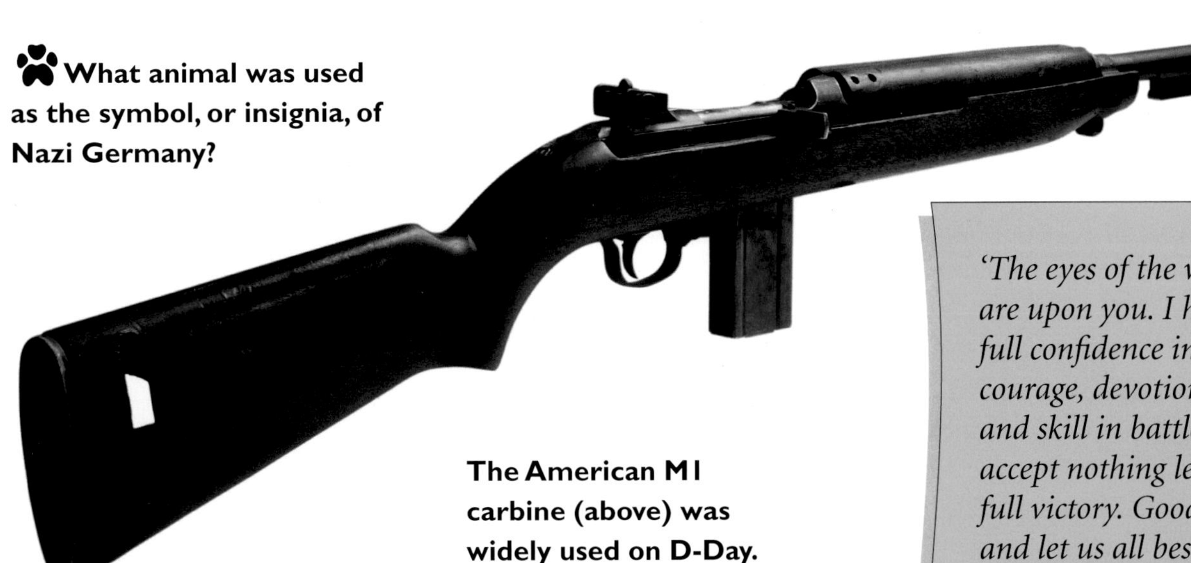

The American M1 carbine (above) was widely used on D-Day.

'The eyes of the world are upon you. I have full confidence in your courage, devotion to duty and skill in battle. We will accept nothing less than full victory. Good luck, and let us all beseech the blessing of Almighty God upon this great and noble undertaking.'

Allied Commander General Eisenhower's address to his troops before the D-Day landing, 6 June 1944.

By D-Day, the troops also carried **submachine guns**, a mix of a machine gun and a pistol that delivered some of the devastating firepower of the machine gun but was far more easy to carry. The main British version was the Sten gun. The American troops carried Thompson or M3 'Grease Guns' (which could fire up to 450 rounds a minute), while the German equivalent was the M34 or M38. Machine guns themselves played a great part in D-Day. Unlike the machine guns used during the First World War – when most of the fighting took place between trenches – Second World War machine guns had to be lighter, like the British Bren gun.

Tanks and aircraft were now playing a major role in warfare. The German Panzer tank units were particularly effective and feared. Luckily for the Allies, by D-Day, the German Panzer units were weakened as the Germans were struggling to replace all the tanks already lost in battle. The importance of tanks gave rise to a whole new range of infantry weapons, designed to destroy tanks at short range. The most famous of these was the German Panzerfaust, introduced in 1942, which shot a high-explosive anti-tank missile through a metal tube.

The M3 'Grease Gun' was a submachine gun that could hit its targets at up to 90 m (300 ft).

What weapons do modern Special Forces use?

During the Second World War, some armies created Special Forces. These were small units with special training for operations that took place behind enemy lines. One of the earliest units was the British Special Air Service (known as the SAS, formed in North Africa in 1941), later joined by units such as the Special Boat Squadron (SBS). Today, Special Forces take part in missions against terrorism, as well as being active in wars around the world.

In the years following the end of the Second World War, deep mistrust developed between the United States and the Soviet Union, known as the Cold War. Each side threatened the other with destruction by **nuclear weapons**, but they did not fight directly. Instead, many smaller-scale wars broke out around the world involving allies of one side or the other, such as the wars in Korea (1951–53) and Vietnam (1959–75).

Detective work

The British SAS hit the newspaper headlines when they stormed an embassy in London to release 26 hostages held there, an event seen on live television. Which country did the embassy belong to? Search on 'Operation Nimrod' at www.eliteukforces.info

A US Special Forces soldier fires an M134 Minigun from a combatant craft.

This assault rifle (left) is fitted with a night-vision scope, so that it can be used in the dark.

To adapt to these new types of smaller-scale warfare, the major armies had to think of new methods. They turned to the special skills – such as reconnaissance (information gathering) and secret attacks on enemy targets – used by Special Forces. Teams such as Delta Force, formed by the United States in 1977, were given a particular mission to work against terrorism.

What colours are the modern army uniforms worn in combat?

Special Forces often use normal army weapons, selecting those most adapted for their particular task. In general, these must be light and reliable, as Special Forces often work far away from their supply bases. Equipment used by the British SAS includes the MPFA5 submachine gun, which can fire around 800 rounds a minute, and Browning high-power pistols. In the US Special Forces, weapons include the M16 assault rifle and the MP7 submachine gun.

Special Forces also use a variety of specialist weapons, including stun grenades (which create explosions that confuse the enemy without harming them) and combat knives. A modern, lightweight form of body armour that can resist bullets is worn for protection in combat.

The MP7 submachine gun (below) is used by units of the German Special Forces.

Your project

Are there any museums in your area with displays of weapons or armour? Castles often have collections of weapons from medieval times, or from the English Civil War in the seventeenth century. Some museums, such as the Royal Armouries in Leeds and London and the Imperial War Museum, have collections of modern weaponry as well.

What periods are covered by the collections in the museum? Do the types of weapons change over time, or are certain sorts of weapons used in more than one period? Find out about the wars in which these weapons were used. Did soldiers wear armour, and if so, of what type? If the conflict was more recent, does the museum have examples of the soldiers' uniforms?

Sometimes groups of people recreate battles of the past. These 're-enactors' try to make their weapons and armour as similar as possible to those used in the actual battle. Are there any re-enactor groups in your area? What period of history do they recreate? If you see a re-enactment, what weapons do they use? Describe a re-enacted battle and what it looks and feels like.

Museums such as the Imperial War Museum in London can give a powerful sense of what it was like to be a soldier in the past, such as a gunner in a First World War trench.

Project presentation

- Archaeologists often find old weapons (or pieces of them) when they dig into the ground at battlefields. Pick a weapon and tell its story. Start with the time that it was made (who made it and why), then say how it came into the hands of a soldier and what happened to it during and after the battle.

- Pick one type of weapon, such as a sword, spear or pistol. Find at least three examples of the weapon over time and look at how it has developed. Does the gun use a different mechanism or type of bullet? Is the sword a different shape?

- Find a suit of medieval armour (or a picture of one). All the different parts of armour have a special name (such as greaves to cover the legs). Find the names of as many parts of the armour as you can.

In this staging of the 1815 Battle of Waterloo, re-enactors have accurately chosen their uniforms and muskets.

As well as seeing ancient Roman weapons and armour at a re-enactment, real artefacts can be viewed in museums around the country.

Glossary

artillery Large guns, which cannot be carried by hand.

barrel The long, tube-shaped part of a gun or cannon.

bayonet A long blade that can be attached to a gun.

BCE 'Before the Common Era'. Used to signify years before the believed birth of Jesus, around 2,000 years ago.

carbine A light, shortened firearm similar to the musket or rifle.

catapult A large weapon with a lever to hurl missiles.

cavalry Soldiers who fight from horseback.

CE 'Common Era'. Used to signify years since the believed birth of Jesus.

chain mail Armour made from small metal rings.

charge A sudden attack in which soldiers rush forwards against the enemy.

feudalism The way society was organised in the Middle Ages. The nobles were given land in exchange for promising military service to the king.

firearm A device that fires small missiles through a controlled explosion.

hand grenade A small bomb thrown by hand.

infantry Soldiers who fight on foot.

knight A respected warrior active during the Middle Ages.

lance A spear-like weapon that is held rather than thrown.

longbow A large bow used particularly by the English in the fourteenth century.

longship A swift, light ship used by Vikings.

mace A heavy club with a metal ball at the end.

mass-produced Made in large quantities, often in a factory.

mechanism A piece of machinery.

Middle Ages The period of European history from about CE 500 to 1450.

musket A gun with a long barrel, used from the sixteenth to the eighteenth centuries.

muzzle The open part of a gun through which the bullet passes when fired.

nuclear weapon A weapon that uses the energy created when atoms split apart or fuse together to create an enormous explosion.

phalanx A unit of infantry in ancient Greece.

pike A long, thrusting spear.

pistol A gun used in one hand.

sabre A light sword with a curved blade.

shaft The long, narrow body of an arrow or spear.

slingshot Missiles hurled from a hand-held sling.

slingsman A soldier who uses a weapon in the form of a loop to hurl small stones or other missiles.

smooth-bored A gun in which the inside of the barrel is not grooved.

submachine gun A light, hand-held machine gun.

volley The shooting of a large number of bullets or arrows at the same time.

Answers

Page 5: They often used bows and arrows or spears to launch high-speed attacks.
Page 7: Officers might be spotted by the special horsehair crests on their helmets.
Page 8: Poorer Vikings used axes because they were made from iron rather than steel, which made them cheaper to produce.
Page 11: As well as many other duties, squires had to help knights dress in their heavy armour.
Page 12: The Mongol horseman's armour and weapons were light, which did not weigh down their small but agile horses.
Page 15: They kept their ammunition in a pouch or box worn on their belt.
Page 16: The samurai and government troops used swords and muskets.
Page 19: The cannon were pulled by horses.
Page 21: The stars represented the Confederate states, which rose to 13 by the end of the war.
Page 23: They wore gas masks to protect themselves from chemical weapons (poison gas).
Page 25: The eagle was the insignia of Nazi Germany (the eagle is still used as a symbol of Germany today).
Page 27: Combat uniforms are usually camouflaged, for example in shades of yellow and brown for wearing in the desert.

Further Information

Books to read

Ancient Weapons by Will Fowler (Southwater 2008)
Arms and Armour by Michèle Byam (Dorling Kindersley 2003)
Soldier by Simon Adams (Dorling Kindersley 2009)
Weapon: A Visual History of Arms and Armour (Dorling Kindersley 2008)
Weapons: Medieval Warfare by Deborah Murrell (World Almanac Library 2008)

Websites

www.castles.me.uk/medieval-weapons.htm
www.militaryfactory.com/ancient-warfare/index.asp
http://inventors.about.com/od/militaryhistoryinventions/a/firearms_2.htm

Note to parents and teachers: Every effort has been made by the publishers to ensure that these websites are suitable for children. However, because of the nature of the Internet, it is impossible to guarantee that the contents of these sites will not be altered. We strongly advise that Internet access is supervised by a responsible adult.

Places to visit

Among the most spectacular collections of arms and armour, and displays about warfare, are:
Royal Armouries Museum, Leeds LS10 1LW
Fort Nelson, nr Portsmouth PO17 6AN
Tower of London EC3N 4AB
Imperial War Museum, London SE1 6HZ

Index

Numbers in **bold** refer to pictures and captions